ℜeJ

I would like to share my utmost appreciation for all of those who have touched my life in one way or another!

Special appreciation for my loved ones, especially my loving

mothers who fostered my imagination and allowed me the

freedom and space to express it!

"By three methods we may learn wisdom: first, by reflection,

which is noblest; second, by imitation, which is easiest; and

third, by experience, which is the most bitter."

Confucius

Aaron Paul Mossett

REFLECTIONS
OF
A
NICE GUY...

©

Aaron Paul Mossett

Reflections of a Nice Guy...

Notes

Aaron Paul Mossett

Reflections of a Nice Guy…

I WISH I had known then, the things that I know now,
the reasons behind the choices: the who, the what, and the how…
I wish I'd even known the difference between being emotionally sick
and the other feeling I experienced, of being deeply **NOSTALGIC**.
Funny, I can recall days that I wished I weren't born,
but I barely recall the pain of my heart being **TORN**…
Perhaps, it's because I got by on small **INTOXICATIONS**,
A HUG AND A KISS, which also led to **INSPIRATION**.
Maybe it was an **AMBROSIAL** selection,
which led to **SURRENDER** or **AN UNTIMELY EXCLAMATION**…
I guess it could have been just an **IDEAL PHASE**,
Making me **READY AND WILLING** to prove that I could make the grade,
So I gave myself a little time before deciding to commit,
forego **THE REPRESENTATIVE**, persona simulare, who cast a false **HEAD DENT**.
I said **HELLO** to **CONTEMPLATION**, seeing all things had a **BOOMERANG** effect.
"What goes around, comes around." Just hadn't come 'round to me, yet.
To attain great love, I had to risk great hurt.
The goal was to remain the nice guy, it's said they'll **BE LEFT THE DIRT**.
Everything goes through changes, and each change has a start,
and so, the next change began with **AARON'S BROKEN HEART**.
WEARY of nicks and cuts caused by **IMMACULATE DECEITS**,
I took **CONSCIOUS COUNSEL** from an **I'MPRISONED** self,
And learned to **SMILE** at small defeats.
I know I'm like **NO MAN ALIVE** in my quest to find **LO QUE TE HAGA FELIZ**,

Aaron Paul Mossett

translation for the non-bilingual: Whatever makes you happy.
So I changed THE NEXT CHAPTER, in TWILIGHT I braved the
UNKNOWN.
For awhile, for my own health, I became UNAVAILABLE.
As for the man I was, at the BAGGAGE CHECK, I HAD TO LET
IT GO,
unlike BACK THEN, no influence from EVERYONE I KNOW.
Embracing ME, MYSELF, AND I and became A KEEPER OF THE
LIGHT,
but from time to time, I still could hear, "YOU DON'T QUALIFY".
Too many confused the RUNAWAY KING in me with N.E.
OTHERGUY,
and some couldn't notice who I was, cause they held their noses too
high.
So I, whose mom was RAISING ABLE found myself WALKING
AWAY,
from a SUBLIME MISS, possible PERFECTION, and even some
OCD.
Some that couldn't risk THE POT for THE MAN; maybe they
assumed it'd be in vane.
Even still, I clung to my goal, seeking EMINENT DOMAIN,
yet, had to go the route of THE INVISIBLE MAN, something a little
twisted,
but as time took its course, me, myself, and I, OUTSTANDING,
no longer sought to be SOMETHING WICKED.
I'd love to share THIS DANCE, with my DREAMGIRL,
who adores I, POET and fool,
whose desire is to overcome with me and not overrule.
No longer governed by the next COIN TOSS, I finally realized that I
SHINE,
my DRIVE more enjoyable cause I've rediscovered my own INNER
CHILD.
Though I strive to be in CONTENTION,

Aaron Paul Mossett

however, what will be will be
"**QUE SERA SERA**", is the saying,
as is, "Gotta stay true to me…"
Hope you appreciate the smile I wear…
Underneath, there's an **URBAN SAMURAI.**
And when he is awaken…
there is **NO MORE MR. NICE GUY**…

Aaron Paul Mossett

Reflections of a Nice Guy...

Notes

Aaron Paul Mossett

Reflections of a Nice Guy...

I Wish

I wish I had noticed:
>Your freshly plucked eyebrows
>Your delicately manicured nails
>Your beautiful new hairstyle

Because I didn't, I apologize.

I wish I had said:
>Baby you look nice today
>Baby I like it when you wear that
>Baby I am proud to be your man

Because I didn't, I apologize.

I wish I had decided:
>That you did love me as much as you claimed
>That I could trust you with my heart
>That I didn't need to leave you

Because I didn't, I apologize.

I wish I didn't:
>Love you so strongly
>Miss you so much
>Hurt you so deeply

Because I did, I truly apologize.

Aaron Paul Mossett

Reflections of a Nice Guy...
Notes

Aaron Paul Mossett

Reflections of a Nice Guy...

Nostalgic

Remember when your smiles were genuine;
I mean, when you were so inclined to be cheerful?
Remember when the relationship elations
lasted longer than the trials and tribulations?
We used to have so much fun…
Now our discussions have no successions,
they are more like emotional outpour.
Now I feel so helpless, so hopeless, so strength less
'cause I just can't uplift your heart, anymore…
No cooking, no clothes, no surprise, no rose:
nothing seems to do it for very long.
Now we both seem so sad,
And we each assume the other is mad,
that may be why I wrote this poem.
I love you so much, I long for you touch,
your tuneful laughs, your warm embraces
and the way the smiles brighten up your face.
I miss the way you giggle,
and when you want to cuddle, the way you wiggle…
It's not like a rabbit, but more like a cat.
Hope that is not hurtful, just sayin' I miss you,
and I truly want those days back…
I feel I have brought to ruin
those times, which I'm persuin',
and I can't seem to forgive myself for that.
By my expressions, my moods, my ever-changin' attitudes,
seems I've multiplied the stresses you feel.
I want to apologize, but I do realize
I've said sorry so much it's unreal…
It leaves me with this foul taste of hopelessness,
because I just don't know what to say or do…

Aaron Paul Mossett

Reflections of a Nice Guy...

I remember when we laughed, joked, smiled and talked,
I remember we did all four just on how someone walked.
I remember I had smiled more than sighed,
I remember I loved you, and many reasons why,
and I remember I wanted to spend my life with you
I hope that if you've forgotten, soon you'll come to remember those
things, too.

Aaron Paul Mossett

Reflections of a Nice Guy...

Notes

Aaron Paul Mossett

TORN

ONE OF A COUPLE FOR MOST OF MY
LIFE
MANY FEMALE FRIENDS, AND EVEN
ONE WIFE
YET STILL, LONELY...
MOST OF MY EXPRESSIONS SMILES,
BRIGHT AND GLOWING
ON SOME OCCASIONS A LAUGH LOUD
AND FLOWING
EVEN THEN, UNHAPPY...
OF AN UNHAPPY UNION; FREE AFTER
SEVEN
AND THESE LAST FEW MONTHS LIKE
HEAVEN
RIGHT NOW, LONGING...
ENTER AN ANGEL; HER ESSENCE IS
INTOXICATING
FOR HER; IT SEEMS THESE SEVEN
YEARS I'VE BEEN WAITING
BUT SUDDENLY, CONFUSED...

Aaron Paul Mossett

Reflections of a Nice Guy...

NOT ONE ORACLE TO QUERY ABOUT
WHAT SHOULD BE DONE
HURTS SO MUCH TO STAY; YET THERE'S
NO PLACE TO RUN
SO PRESENTLY, BEGUILED...
ALL I WANT; A HEART AND MIND FREE
AND CLEAR
THIS UNEASY FEELING IS MUCH TOO
SEVERE
BECAUSE INSIDE, TORN.

Aaron Paul Mossett

Reflections of a Nice Guy...

Notes

Aaron Paul Mossett

Intoxications

dismal and low of mood,
that's how my day began.
inebriated so much by hymns and the melodies,
I found I could hardly stand.

listening to slow songs,
creating works through blurred lenses;
as my intoxication increased,
my world skewed by the un-sobered senses.

through the melodic, but muddled den
a voice was heard clear and well,
but because of the heady euphony
veracity I could not tell…

a sorry condition, when we met,
and many times when we were together.
perhaps, the rapture that I vent
may be too much for her to weather…

she offered to come by,
to lend me human feel,
first, I declined, then I resigned
'cause I felt her sincerity was real.

she arrived at about four,
I remained imbibed on her presence.
her scent I consumed, deeply,
more potent than 151, was her essence.

Now, I have a hangover

Aaron Paul Mossett

Reflections of a Nice Guy...

for which there is no remedy.
save to stay under the influence of her smile
and that is just fine with me!

Aaron Paul Mossett

Reflections of a Nice Guy...

Notes

Aaron Paul Mossett

a hug and a kiss

he desired a hug; he longed for a kiss
with either one; he knew he'd have bliss
warmth of the body; softness of the lips
little to him was nicer; than a hug and a kiss
a lasting torso embrace; a brief lip caress
with the right woman it'd be simply marvelous
soon he found his right one; their bosoms did they press
a salutation filled with; naught but tenderness
he delighted in enfolding her; his neck so near her face
and as the clinch would loosen; her smile his lips would graze
in some time the endearment lingered; and the cuddle did not regress
they periodically saw each other; the time they shared, the best
he knew he'd fall for her; the first nestle, that "sunny" day
and the day that gentle peck came; he yearned falling all the way
she's the sunshine for him; in light and in darkness
and it all began with a desire for a hug
and the longing for a kiss...

Aaron Paul Mossett

Reflections of a Nice Guy...

Notes

Aaron Paul Mossett

Reflections of a Nice Guy...

inspiration

your are the inspiration of my poems
the first thought when love songs
are heard late night in the streets

you are the beat in my heart
and your smile makes it start
your laugh provides all the heat

I'm inspired by your stride
other women step aside
in recognition of the elite

you are the love in my poems
the sweet in my heart
the pride in my stride
it's all true

but you're some other things
and 'cause I love you, queen
I need to convey these things, too

you are the militant in my mind
which makes me question why
people do the dumb shit they do

you are the strength in my will
with you I do what I feel
within law and in taboo

you are the conscience that guides me
the jockey that rides me

Aaron Paul Mossett

Reflections of a Nice Guy...

pushing me to my peak

you are the sun in my day
the ink on my page
you make me a masterpiece

for this and more
I love and adore, you
you wonderful, lovely lady!

Aaron Paul Mossett

Reflections of a Nice Guy...
Notes

Aaron Paul Mossett

Ambrosial

he was filled with delight;
whenever she was in sight,
and the smell of her
did not but refresh.
the stroke of her touch, solace
he was captivated by her sound,
she made him leap and bound,
keeping her in focus as he gave chase;
the inducement,
her lips he might taste.
she enchanted all senses.
even his mind had no fences;
he could comprehend the absolute universe.
she gave his heart song.
lifting him where he belonged;
for that he'd forever be grateful.
she made his nature not ever spiteful.
in fact, it was perpetually sunlight full.
though his soul called her love;
his body ever hailed her, Delightful!

Aaron Paul Mossett

Reflections of a Nice Guy...

Notes

Aaron Paul Mossett

Reflections of a Nice Guy...

surrender

I call this one surrender,
but not as is in retreat;
although that is what my mind said,
when first we did meet.

both of us intelligent,
so thinkers then are we;
but to the will of my heart,
I had no choice but concede.

to the thrill of your presence,
to the warmth of your touch,
to you, my smiling innocence
did I, timidly, entrust.

after months of settling for good,
these last moons, with you, have been best;
to the thought of you stimulating that joy,
I am inclined to acquiesce.

the ultimate act of a warrior,
is to lay down his steel;
thus in your virtuous presence,
my alter ego, Black, did yield.

You have made Chumley more active,
consequently, Aaron affirms to feeling more bliss;
to whatever it is about you,
We, all three of us, humbly, submit.

be it your smile, your laugh,

Aaron Paul Mossett

Reflections of a Nice Guy...

talk, walk, even your attempts to play dumb;
Your benevolence and of course intelligence,
to it all, I, yours truly, succumb...

Aaron Paul Mossett

Reflections of a Nice Guy...

Notes

Aaron Paul Mossett

Reflections of a Nice Guy...

an untimely exclamation

a wondrous day, as she came into sight
she had finally arrived, his angel in flight
greeted with a hug, a precipitated interpolation…

within the hour they were seated, a table of two
"you were dearly missed," and "I missed you, too."
he loved her for that, her premier vociferation…

later that evening, they viewed an adoration event
they paused it sometimes to discuss what was meant
the story itself, an unanticipated insinuation…

in darkness of night, he laid down beside her
his desire to know her, he could no longer defer
too late he realized, his overhasty interjection…

later he kicked himself for his cavernous oversight
his true feelings were made unclear, and he couldn't get right
cause of an untimely exclamation…

he wanted to beg her for one more time
he silently pleaded with his wayward mind
"Why now?! Why such an impulsive eruption?!"

his pride wouldn't allow a beg or a plead
for any of the time he thought he would need
to correct his immature declaration…

through her thoughtful sobriety
he began to taste his male impropriety
becoming increasingly unsettled at his unripe expelation…

Aaron Paul Mossett

Reflections of a Nice Guy...

for here he was, his intimate debut
and in her eyes he saw his revue:
"Headliner stumbles over premature ejaculation!"

Aaron Paul Mossett

Reflections of a Nice Guy...

Notes

Aaron Paul Mossett

Ideal Phase

as I enjoy this beautiful daze
listening to jazz
while in a bewitching haze
I am aware of the angel beside
me
eyes, does her grace amaze
hearing her laugh
sets my heart ablaze
I am sunny about this seraph heaven sent
me
adoration for her can naught but raise
considering her friendship
it gets naught but praise
I am rich 'cause this jewel can be touched by
me
happiness, around her stays
watching her sleep
cannot break my gaze
I am slow to wake from this dream, but don't pinch
me
love for her tends to glaze
waxing for her day-by-day
feels when she's ready, it will be emblazed
I am claimed by this treasure, soundly!

Aaron Paul Mossett

Reflections of a Nice Guy...

Notes

Aaron Paul Mossett

ready and willing?

Leave her alone?
Give her some space?
For this, is she ready?
Slow down the pace?

She warned you before,
you should notice another.
She doesn't know if she's ready
for one like you to love her.

Yeah, she may like you,
and may even grow to be smitten.
But her heart just ain't ready.
In the stars it's not yet written.

She's consistently reminding you
that she's confused and unmoored.
To give you love, she's not ready
but you deserve to be adored...

So, why do you fall
for these women, ill-advised?
Their hearts never ready,
therefore reciprocation seldom realized.

You wish you could bury deep, this,
your bleeding heart,
because it's not yet ready
for the prick of Cupid's dart.

You wonder if she knows,

Aaron Paul Mossett

Reflections of a Nice Guy...

your heart she is stealing…
You'd guard hers with your life
if commit it to you, she was willing,
but it just doesn't seem to be ready…

Aaron Paul Mossett

Reflections of a Nice Guy...

Notes

Aaron Paul Mossett

Reflections of a Nice Guy...

The Representative

The representative is a person
who acts in the stead of another…
You'll usually meet the rep
in the first impressions of a potential lover.
They say the right things,
they perform the ideal actions,
they do whatever they believe
will elicit the happiest reactions.
They have the act down, so well
it's like they've perfected the science.
Then the warranty runs out,
like an old household appliance.
It just ain't the same, anymore.
They no longer do what they did back then.
Leaving us to ask ourselves,
"How in the hell did they keep that shit hidden?!"
Well, it's the game of the rep,
their practice is intense,
then they play for the score,
and give high fives to their rep friends;
and now there's a new breed out:
their goal is to gain control.
They have better staying power than the older model,
at least, 'til you develop a mind of your own.
These reps have a knack
for exploiting sincerity and affection,
but a stronger sense of self
may be your surest protection.
Self will tell you, "Something's off, my friend!"
"All ain't what is seems to be!"
"It ain't a good idea," Self will warn,

Aaron Paul Mossett

Reflections of a Nice Guy...

"...extendin' this warranty!"
The assurance will expire
and yes, it will leave a foul feeling,
but be comforted that you were spared more distress
because the rep has left the building...

Aaron Paul Mossett

Reflections of a Nice Guy...

Notes

Aaron Paul Mossett

Head Dent

as he sat there pondering
"what do I do next?"
his mind was distracted
by images of kissed necks.
soft lips and smooth skin
prolong the abstraction.
his mind, so totally befuddled,
that his body fell short of action.
he tried to clear his head,
but it all went kinda wrong.
he hoped she wasn't thinking,
"That didn't last very long…"
he tried to absolve it
thinking, "It's happened to everyone."
but this was his head dent.
this was his first impression.
it began substantially,
but then it was done.
it might as well have been over
before it had ever begun.
there was no, "Ooh!"
there was no, "Damn!"
there was no begging for redemption,
he just wasn't that type of man
to withdrawn and inhibited, from a came and a went
insubstantial first impression: a fine Head Dent

Aaron Paul Mossett

Reflections of a Nice Guy...

Notes

Aaron Paul Mossett

Reflections of a Nice Guy...

Hello?

Hey there, how're you doing?
It's nice to hear from you again.
To be honest, I was beginning to wonder,
if we were still considering ourselves friends.
I think when last we spoke,
we were at a sort of quandary…
The thing I understood, though,
was I needed to let you be.
So I began to do my own thing,
knowing that you would do you;
you always were on my mind, though.
I truly hope you knew.
So please remember, always
or, at least, 'til I tell you again,
you'll always be in my heart,
as a true and most special friend…

Aaron Paul Mossett

Reflections of a Nice Guy...

Notes

Aaron Paul Mossett

Contemplation

Sitting in darkness
Looking into myself
Some may say waisting time
So be it, I have that, in wealth
I listen to a sad melody
The sax plays my mind's mood
wine glass to my right
Melancholy is my food
Long moments do I dine
Then I begin to write
Hoping the action will hasten
Another lonely night
Time spent scripting thoughts
Same as other nights before
Evolves to a night of sleeplessness
Wondering what tomorrow has in store
Hate to think I'm alone,
in this, depth of solitude
Guiltily comforted in the thought
Elsewhere, in the world, another likely broods
I want to cure this sadness
Find joy within myself
Find happiness in the person I am
Not entirely in someone else
But it's all so ironic
The goal is also the rub
Cause I wish to share my
I feel incomplete without a love…

Aaron Paul Mossett

Reflections of a Nice Guy...
Notes

Aaron Paul Mossett

Boomerang

the smooth operator, was himself
a trick of the trade
his mind was on the women
his strut was on parade
with his words he invited
with his smile he entranced
opening countless doorways
for his subtle advances
roses deflowered
but never left wilting
eventually he began to feel
this enterprise was unfulfilling
retiring his black book
he decided to settle
but in this decision
karma would meddle
he met quite the lady
his expectations she exceeded
"be mine," "stay mine."
he begged and he pleaded
she stayed out of his reach
for just long enough
the two of them were contrived, it seemed,
from the same sort of stuff
she hesitated for a while
and he began to cleave
so for the next days that followed
she ducked, bobbed, and weaved
when finally cornered, she calmly injected
"I am sorry, Sweetie, but I'm not so affected."
with that said, she turned and went

Aaron Paul Mossett

leaving him quite dejected.
To put it simply, for those who have no retrospect,
few laws are more strict
than the law of cause and effect...

Aaron Paul Mossett

Reflections of a Nice Guy...

Notes

Aaron Paul Mossett

be left the dirt

those in Entech resigned
those in the NFL re-signed
I'm just trying to get mine
but constantly on my mind
how can I be on an N team?
to get my piece of the big dream
or must I dream of the big peace
haven't owned, but rented to…
am I an aspiring spirit, or a zealous fool
those in political office resign
those on the NBA re-sign
oops, did I just rewind
well these things on my mind
eternally marked, I am
deeply scarred, the Ram
a brother of Mars
that's an Aries
full of anger, passion, and heat
never admit to defeat
but I am one of the meek
supposedly, one who will acquire the turf
ha, for some reason that brings me mirth
that means it's laughable
'cause nice guys do finish last, I'm told
I wish I could recast the role
but nice guy I be
still desiring to see
that being a good guy is worth it all
but I feel I've been thrown a moral screwball
that's a fucked up pitch
'cause being nice hasn't established my worth

Aaron Paul Mossett

Reflections of a Nice Guy...

and if I can't acquire the land
how will I inherit the Earth?

Aaron Paul Mossett

Reflections of a Nice Guy...

Notes

Aaron Paul Mossett

Aaron's Broken Heart

Love breaks the heart, confuses the brain, and pains the soul;
among the three, only one wanted its role
and the heart
well it was at the center of it all.

The brain wished it didn't think so much;
the soul woed ever being so touched
and the heart
well it never remembered being broken.

The brain had come to the end of its wit;
the soul just wanted no more of that shit
and the heart
well it went by the beat of its own thump.

The brain and the soul agreed to come up with a plan;
they would devise a defense to save the spirit of this man
and the heart
well it only wanted to love.

The brain would distract until love was sure;
the soul agreed, for that seemed to be the best cure
and the heart
well it went on the attack.

The brain and the soul could not understand;
what was wrong with their love delay plan
well the heart
it had decided to fall in love at its own pace.

Aaron Paul Mossett

Reflections of a Nice Guy...

Notes

Aaron Paul Mossett

Reflections of a Nice Guy...

weary

weary of this heartache,
this headache, and this stomach ache; three
pains I get, when I'm sick of wanting to be free

weary of not wanting to go home,
cause I know you're there
just be hopin' you're sleep, of me, unaware

weary of your anger,
it's like a boiling room
I might dry out if you don't get happy soon.

weary of battling you, daily
cause I don't know what to do, lately
but something's just got to give

weary of these trials and tribulations,
and their momentary elations,
it's like being repeatedly dropped from a cliff

weary of your apologies
and your tearless pleas
when you grudgingly admit you were wrong

weary of my love for you
that feeling which gets me through
all of the issues in this poem

weary of being teary eyed
I mean just plain sick and tired
of feeling ire, from thinking of this stuff for so long

Aaron Paul Mossett

Reflections of a Nice Guy...

weary of you claiming to love me
evidence I very rarely see
just another reason why I wrote this poem

weary of this hurt that I feel
it recurs like a classic movie reel
in fact, it's time for a monologue

weary of the knowledge that
no matter what I do or say
in the end, the bottom line is:
I'm going to love you anyway…

Aaron Paul Mossett

Reflections of a Nice Guy...

Notes

Aaron Paul Mossett

Immaculate deceits

This ain't the way it's supposed to be:
Me lovin you,
you playin' me.

If you found another, let him fill my shoes.
I'm in love with you,
yet you givin' me the blues.

That's incorrect? Please, tell what I should see?
Now it's you talkin' to him for two hours,
when you were supposed to call me...

When I ask you later, "Why didn't you call?"
I get your half-assed-truth,
"I'm sorry. I got sleepy, that's all..."

Yet, you were on the phone with him, giving him my time
guess I no longer rate so much,
I'm just a two-minute dime...

As good as I try to treat you, the mountains I'd climb,
the flames I've jumped for you,
they should call me the paradigm!

I do look out for you and I'm loved by your fam...
But, seems, you'd rather spend time
with a lesser man...

Naivety like mine, wouldn't have gone on, I'm sure.
The break-up due to this,
I'm sure will endure.

Aaron Paul Mossett

Reflections of a Nice Guy...

I hope you see this.
I pray you realize.
I loved you so much.
But, I hated those white lies!

Aaron Paul Mossett

Reflections of a Nice Guy...

Notes

Aaron Paul Mossett

Conscious counsel

now you've done it,
and all feels lost.
you've fallen in love,
what will be the cost?
a broken heart?
some plundered emotions?
complicated expectations?
misguided devotions?
you were supposed to remain friends.
she warned you she may not be right.
you tried to stay aloof,
it was a futile fight.
so what do you do now?
you can sit back and enjoy the climb.
it could be the best roller coaster ever,
one without a decline.
yeah a few looptee loops.
even some twists and turns,
for the ride to never end
that's what you really yearn.
but everything changes
nothing remains the same.
so enjoy what there is to enjoy
allow those memories to remain.
I know you care for her
and it' s rough not knowing what's due
I will always remind:
"There will be someone for you!"
until then, enjoy your fun
for as long as you can,
treat her like she's the one!

Aaron Paul Mossett

Reflections of a Nice Guy...

Notes

Aaron Paul Mossett

I'm Prisoned

I am a caged man.
Though no bars do I see,
For I am jailed by my doubts
and likely a few insecurities.
Don't know if I am good enough.
Can't tell if my thoughts are right.
An angel with the strongest wings,
who balks at the highest heights.
I've climbed my life's mountains,
though rarely to their peaks.
Just close enough to feel I'm able,
that's routinely where my trek will cease.
I ask, "What if I'm not good enough?"
I question if my pride is false.
For an ego being so affected,
is not likely to survive such falls.
I am a caged man.
It's not the way I want to be,
so, I'm training myself to fly or plunge,
either way, my aim is to be free!

Aaron Paul Mossett

Reflections of a Nice Guy...

Notes

Aaron Paul Mossett

smile

her smile has brightened the world I exist in
I'd give one eye to see it again
her laugh provided harmony which my life surly needed
if not for experiencing it myself, I would not have believed it
if I were dumb, deaf, and blind, she could not be ignored
'cause when she smiled my way, it warmed me to the core
my joy is supported with her smile's assistance
as if my heart looks upon her through rose colored lenses
my mind shrugs off sadness at her laugh's sincere tone
and the memory brings me company even when I'm alone
it's helped me find something I had not seen in awhile
a desire in myself to share my own smile

Aaron Paul Mossett

Reflections of a Nice Guy...

Notes

Aaron Paul Mossett

no man alive

don't think you will ever be content,
you couldn't keep a smile if it was heaven sent.
it must be in your blood to find complaint,
if it were up to you; Valentine wouldn't be a saint.
your folk tried to dissuade me, but I ignored the warning,
so they just shook their heads at my 'love for you' story.
with a smile on their faces,
a pat on my back,
and words amongst themselves;
"I hope he can hack."
call it false confidence, better yet foolish pride.
hell, even your baby's daddy stated you'd be happy…
with no man alive
they're all outsiders, they don't know you like I do
I should get through any difficulties, just 'cause I have so much love
for you.
but whenever I think that, I fear for a split
commenced with the line, "What's love got to do with it?"
I guess it's redundant, and it makes you, "so tired"
I wish you knew how that line gets me wired.
we're in the same relationship, yet you're more tired than I,
and it seems more and more like you're too tired to try.
but I hang in there. I struggle and strive,
not all men would do this,
maybe no man alive
so now a new mantra has become less rare,
day in night out I repeat, "I don't even care."
it's the effect of futility, the by-product of restraint,
model of inexhaustibility, guess that's what I ain't.
I'm weary of my compromise, when it seems that you won't,
I tire of my sacrifice, when it seems that you don't.

Aaron Paul Mossett

Reflections of a Nice Guy...

if his woman's happiness can be a litmus for a man's success
then I've got to be failing the "you are a man, now" test.
so I guess I'm doomed to be a boy 'til I die,
cause I continue to be no man, alive.

Aaron Paul Mossett

Reflections of a Nice Guy...

Notes

Aaron Paul Mossett

Reflections of a Nice Guy...

lo que te haga feliz...

since the beginning of our time,
I've wanted for your gladness.
maybe, hopefully through this rhythm,
you'll understand my madness.

when I said I loved you,
and I wanted you to be happy,
I truly, truly desired
all that compelled your glee.

so I proffered to cede my bliss for yours,
on more than one occasion;
not because I wanted out
because, I wanted your elation.

you aspired to be a better mother
I said, "I'll step aside."
I thought my presence stressful
so I chose to take the ride...

I claim I want you happy
and hope you feel that's true,
even if that happiness means
someone else for you.

so tell me the things he does,
the things that I neglected;
cause by these things, even the little things
is your happiness affected.

when you said you admired him

Aaron Paul Mossett

Reflections of a Nice Guy...

I was glad for your delight,
although I cringed at the thought,
I truly took no slight.

I guess you hadn't considered all,
when you said you wanted to stay friends.
I thought that meant being there for each other,
for life's out and life's ins…

so about any of my joy,
no more will you hear a peep
regrettably, I refer to your spoken words
"I hope that helps you sleep…"

for a friendship with me,
you say you're not yet ready,
to that I'll reply, discordantly,
lo que te haga feliz…

Aaron Paul Mossett

Reflections of a Nice Guy...

Notes

Aaron Paul Mossett

the next chapter
well it has been confirmed,
though it took some time
it is actually done,
there will be no denying
in this book called, "My Life",
a chapter has been concluded
everything is written out clearly,
so no one feels deluded
there was no need to soothe,
there was no want to gloss
no ill-will and no regrets,
concerning what time had been lost
now I move along,
to "My Life's" next phase,
and I'm starting from scratch
on an empty page
nothing at all is marked,
only margins are defined
as for anything else,
there's not even an outline
there is no thesis,
there is no theme
only a jumble of thoughts
something of a waking dream
within this cognition,
there is no delicate scene
a prominent desire:
from myself, sensitivity wean
for some excellent mate,
there is no consonant plea
the one sure idea about this chapter…
the main character is finally me.

Aaron Paul Mossett

Reflections of a Nice Guy...

Notes

Aaron Paul Mossett

Twilight

He'd felt sunshine before
For months it brought his daze
It made his heart blossom
Shining through gloomy haze
He constantly desired this sunshine
From when he woke until he slept
But through his dreams he glimpsed reality
The light was to be admired, never kept
But feeling such delightful warmth
More sunshine he sincerely craved
But due to his own internal clouds
The brightness could not be saved
After a time the shine began to dim
The colors his days would lack
Consequently without that sunshine
His world eventually faded to black....

Aaron Paul Mossett

Reflections of a Nice Guy...

Notes

Aaron Paul Mossett

Reflections of a Nice Guy...

unknown

he had thought he was losing his hold
he'd thought about having himself committed
because he wanted to cry and laugh simultaneously
he was like a genius that had been un-witted
for he had this grand idea
and he was dying to share his soul
but if he spoke the lines he wished to
the entire script could un-role
it seemed as long as the parts were strictly played
the action was all games and fun
however, he'd have liked to improvise a bit
but the whole play may have been undone
until that point, the act had entertained so many
especially the main players involved
not necessarily a whodunit, more so a who-will-do-it
but still, that mystery remained unsolved
there was a line or action missing
and nothing known to satisfy the task
until he found a means to fill the void
the bit remained un-cast
without that role, he had an incomplete cast
thus, his production may never be shown
without his wits, he had an incomplete solution
thus, his masterpiece may forever be unknown

Aaron Paul Mossett

Reflections of a Nice Guy...

Notes

Aaron Paul Mossett

Unavailable
Hello? No, he's not in right now.
No, I'm not sure where he went.
No, I don't know when he'll return.
I haven't heard from or seen him since.
Well, I can tell you that when he left,
he didn't seem quite himself.
But when I asked him what was on his mind,
he never said how he felt.
Actually, he's been gone awhile now;
I would say like a few days.
Between me and you,
he was gone before he ever left this place.
See before he physically left,
it seemed his mind had gone away.
When did you last speak to him?
Hmm, it began around that day.
For several days, though hungry,
he said he couldn't eat.
For several nights, though exhausted,
he continually refused to sleep.
When the telephone rang for him,
he didn't want to talk;
and you know how he loves to drive;
well for days all he did was walk.
So, when you last spoke to him,
you implied there might be need for space?
Well that explains at least one thing,
the look of loss upon his face.
Well, don't you worry too much, honey,
I'm sure he'll be okay.
And after he's figured this thing out;
I'm sure he'll call you back some day…

Aaron Paul Mossett

Reflections of a Nice Guy...

Notes

Aaron Paul Mossett

Baggage Check

When embarking on new connections
each of us comes with his/her own past.
However, some of us fuck up flight plans
attempting to carry on check-in bags.
Folks are shouldering knock-off luggage,
shit that shouldn't be on any plane;
some of the stuff is so emotionally heavy,
that it puts wrinkles on the brain.
Folks having stresses and flashbacks
as a result of events on a previous trip;
so now, if he smiles at a stewardess,
we may see Ms. Insecure just flip.
Or if she's ready to fly, he balks, with claims like:
"My flight five years ago involved some bumpy air…"
Inspector Clouseau type conjecture,
check that shit at the entrance, *mon frère*!
That check-in type slough has us tripping,
stuck on preceded and presumed transgressions;
most things, are understood, and we'll help bear:
offspring, business, learned and unlearned lessons…
By carrying on all that check-in baggage,
folks allow for limited headway;
maybe if you leave some of that stuff at the check-in,
a good person can sit in its place…
But continue to carry on check-in baggage,
expecting others to take it, happily, and with pains;
lug that shit to the boarding gate, and see the flight en route
meanwhile, in the terminal, you and your baggage remain, un-
claimed…

Aaron Paul Mossett

Reflections of a Nice Guy...

Notes

Aaron Paul Mossett

Had to let it go

I relayed how I felt about her,
It wasn't the same ever since.
I felt that she washed her hands of me,
All that was left to do was rinse.
I really believed I loved her,
Just ask anyone I know.
But due to some implications,
I was inclined to let her go.
I think it made it easier for her,
me to come to that resolution;
to allay any guilt she might ever feel.
She could claim it was my want.
Can't say that I am mad at her,
I'm just a little struck.
Guess it's better while emotions are somewhat neat,
Rather than if they'd been amuck.
Well so long, aufwiedersehn, goodbye
I had to let it go
That delightful butterfly....

Aaron Paul Mossett

Reflections of a Nice Guy...

Notes

Aaron Paul Mossett

Back Then

I was that kid
>	The one that comes to school with thoughts of being alone
>	The one whose main goal all day is to get back home
>	Not because home life is much better than outside
>	But, inside there are no clowns or bullies who poke and chide
I was that kid
>	The one whose social skills are not quite right
>	The one who has to defend himself,
>	with quietness or quickness to fight.
>	I didn't have the temperament to change the issue.
I was that kid
>	The one who can make others laugh
>	The one on the inside who's terribly sad
>	and you still don't know the half

of it let me enlighten you:
young black male frustrated and mad
couldn't understand why my life seemed so sad
putting on airs, like all was good and fine
the distress was immeasurable when viewed through my eyes
even now, the grief is foul; but it was constant
everyday
I felt weak, all looked bleak
I needed one brighter day
my mama's eldest child
no daddy around so I ran wild
lost in the mix, never had a fix
at least, not until the Y2K
tried no to disrespect on any given day
but always impatient, so
"Move bitch get out the way!"

Aaron Paul Mossett

Reflections of a Nice Guy...

but then I regressed, fell back into the pit
of melancholy, depression, and other bullshit
until one day someone chose to help
though I made it tough for their assistance
I knew I couldn't do it myself
so here I am still alive
surviving day to day, hoping to thrive
I've taken more control of life
each action an attempt to be correct
I make good causes, hoping for good effects
No longer experiencing severe strife
Conversely, I am starting to enjoy life.

Aaron Paul Mossett

Reflections of a Nice Guy...

Notes

Aaron Paul Mossett

Everyone I know...

Everyone I know has my shoulder to cry on...
Everyone I know has my ear to bend...
Everyone I know has my hand to hold...
Everyone I know has my word to depend...
Everyone I know has my laugh to cheer...
Everyone I know has my empathy to expect...
Everyone I know has my smile to warm...
Everyone I know has my hug to protect...
Everyone I know has my heart to love him or her...
Everyone I know has someone like me, but me.

Aaron Paul Mossett

Reflections of a Nice Guy...

Notes

Aaron Paul Mossett

Me, Myself, I

Me
The curse of the eternal smile
No time to cry, no good reason to frown
In my shoes, you try that mile
And then, perhaps you will see
At times it's the way I like to be…

Myself
Doing good deeds, playing the square
Now living by karmic rulez
But in my youth, I took all dares
Grew up in the hood, one of a coterie
Sometimes it's the way I need to be…

I
Endured pains where other men stammered
Yet I remain the consummate romantic
Still desire the disposition enamored
It's easily natural, this heart on my sleeve
Most times it's the way I want to be.

Aaron Paul Mossett

Reflections of a Nice Guy...

Notes

Aaron Paul Mossett

a keeper of the light

he was getting tired of giving people niceties
for which they were never gracious.
when he offered delight, they sought ill will;
rather than his light, they wanted his shadiness.
he didn't want to admit it,
but he was ever casting his pearls before swine.
he didn't quite know how to cease it,
so his splendor, he continued to consign.
consequently, they persisted
in taking his kindness as a weakness.
never fully understanding,
exploratory, was his meekness.
his un-designed self, the man he'd rather avoid being,
would put people in a spot where they had no place to go,
while he knew all along, they would rather die before fleeing.
but he began to fall back into that old divergence.
the villain; just a few weeks of character overhaul
hell, why be Prince Charming
when everyone wanted Baron Disenthrall?
he sat back and considered the depth that his descent could reach,
"you'll be sorry, foolish mortals!"
he thought to himself, smiling wickedly.
not quite evil; just a foil to his agreeable self: unenlightening,
uninspiring,
and unremarkable. Shit, the dude was bland.
he would no longer greet with laughter or smile,
instead he'd just nod or wave a hand.
some began to wonder;
as to the decline in his enchantment,
others realized immediately,
his usual radiance was unmistakably non-attendant.

Aaron Paul Mossett

Reflections of a Nice Guy...

not long after, among those who knew of him
a considerable sadness had emanated.
and for those that knew him closely,
the bleakness was exacerbated.
and woe to the folk
upon whom his interests had been projected,
for they didn't understand
how, by his glow, they had been so affected.
but understanding finally dawned,
as he receded out of sight:
how can you recognize the end of the tunnel
if you neglect the one who tends the light?

Aaron Paul Mossett

Reflections of a Nice Guy...
Notes

Aaron Paul Mossett

you don't qualify

while others went ahead,
he had no choice but remain behind,
studying the bold faced words:
"you must be this tall to ride."
so he turned away with a sigh,
seeing himself, i don't qualify…
he got a little taller
so in football he wished to back the line
but the coach always fronted him:
"you need to gain some more size,"
he turned away with a sigh,
considering himself, i don't qualify…
he grew more inches and put on some weight.
attractive women began to bend his eyes.
but with one line his heart they'd break,
"sorry, but, you're just too nice,"
he turned away with a sigh,
berating himself, i don't qualify…
things of that sort pained him little,
once alleviated by self-pride.
he kept a mantra in his head:
"don't sweat the small stuff, and it's all small, right?"
very little was big enough to turn his plans awry
all else was addressed, "you don't qualify."
after instances of rejection, discontent, and heartbreak,
he finally figured, "the way I am, is just fine!"
a paraphrase no longer let him be marred:
"cast no iridescence before the porcine"
consequently, he would turn away, no longer sharing his shine
thinking to himself, you don't qualify…

Aaron Paul Mossett

Reflections of a Nice Guy...

Notes

Aaron Paul Mossett

runaway king

she called me a runaway king
not an escapee from some demesne
nor a man of extravagant means,
a maturing prince, never been libertine

my kingdom would be called Adoration
my one liege would be queen,
naught would be her capitation,
save honesty, courtesy, of course, fair exchange

she claimed I was a coveted monarch,
without doubt I would achieve my reign,
but I must find in myself adulation,
so in search of mine own joy, I ran

to make others happy had been my dynasty
with a change of my mind I began,
more self-content, I desired to be
and acknowledge the majesty of my lifespan.

she called me a runaway king
she meant a type of wanted man
to relish myself; my new theme
thus recognize the king that I am.

Aaron Paul Mossett

Reflections of a Nice Guy...

Notes

Aaron Paul Mossett

Reflections of a Nice Guy...

N.E. Otherguy

there is tale of a man
though his existence seems to mystify,
sometimes referred to as Never Exceptional
but more widely known as N. E. Otherguy.
of him, many men have heard
but none claim, or want, to be him
I am beginning to believe,
perhaps, only women can see him
he's mainly brought up at times,
when I'm being less than aggressive,
though I remember at one point,
my manners were considered impressive.
I take pride in having respect for women,
I love that I exhibit some class,
but from what I've heard of this Otherguy,
he's flippant, roughneck, and makes it obvious he really wants the ass.
This may be how other men respond to her,
I treat her like a lady, there is no game,
so maybe it's due to her ego,
that she's compelled to voice the N.E. Otherguy claim.
I've never been a spineless man,
I'll stand up to her or any other, if there's need,
but, I refuse to fight for small things,
which includes her ego's greed.
Yes, I may be a very nice guy,
willing to treat a lady like she's royal,
but she's truly got me fucked up,
if she believes I'll needlessly toil.
And as for my libido,
I do my thing: car, floor, chair, or bed,
but my aim is to please utilizing all my weapons,

Aaron Paul Mossett

not just wielding the lower head.
So to you who know men like me,
about to shove them aside,
keep in mind that every indiscriminate man,
is capable of being N. E. Otherguy.
Apparently, this Otherguy was something,
I don't pretend to know what that involved,
well if there's an answer to the riddle,
it has yet to be truly solved.
Here is the enigmatic question,
the one that clouds my mind:
If the dude is still something of a standard,
why ain't she with N.E. Otherguy?

Aaron Paul Mossett

Reflections of a Nice Guy...

Notes

Aaron Paul Mossett

Raising Able

She knew she had been preceded by others,
those young single black women
trying to raise young brothers.
Yet she still wondered if she would succeed.

She had witnessed her father raise her brothers.
It did not look easy,
even with help, her mother's.
So alone, what chance did she have?

Now it was more than ten years after.
New dangers were present.
So many avenues toward potential disaster,
yet, still she moved forward.

She taught him it was imperative to persevere.
She told him don't run home from a fight,
or she'd meet him at the door, show him true fear.
He learned to press on.

Through her he learned that knowledge was power.
She made books readily available.
Of his early discipline, she was the endower.
He developed a desire for education.

A child, it takes a village to raise;
though she had siblings and parents,
her son gave her most praise.
He fostered a deep respect for strong women.

She taught him life was not always fair,

Aaron Paul Mossett

Reflections of a Nice Guy...

but you should always give your best,
all else you just had to grin and bear.
He sustained a strong sense of justice.

At times she wasn't the model of niceness,
but as he came of age,
he understood well, her sacrifices.
Through them he learned how to love.

Young single black woman, whose dreams had to wait,
having the child at the time would be argued;
but in the end none could debate.
She had raised a very good man!

Aaron Paul Mossett

Reflections of a Nice Guy...

Notes

Aaron Paul Mossett

walking away

I'm walking away, now
Giving you plenty of room
As for your interest in me
I will no longer presume
So, I'm walking away, now
For me to stay, I expect no plea
Truthfully, how could I
You previously implied that "we" couldn't be
So, I'm walking away, now
And each step gets more steady
Braving this road without you
Won't claim that I'm ready
Still, I'm walking away, now
Approaching a new dawn
When the sun has risen, again
I will be truly gone…

Aaron Paul Mossett

Reflections of a Nice Guy...

Notes

Aaron Paul Mossett

Reflections of a Nice Guy...

Sublime Miss(Perfect Lady)

brilliantly glowing; her personality
abundantly flowing
she embodied his bliss
of her he was quite fond; her friendship
he yearned to go beyond
just one simple kiss
splendidly evaded; her indication
discarded left him elated
desiring to be in her midst
excellently eluded; her attendance
never diluted
readily reminisced
a warm embrace; her design
a lovely face
he could not resist
that gorgeous female; her appearance
preceded an eminent farewell
the ambiguity; a sublime miss...

Aaron Paul Mossett

Reflections of a Nice Guy...

Notes

Aaron Paul Mossett

Perfection

Perfection is slow death.
Hugh Prather said that.
Now, he must have been a man who met nine out of ten
things on the perfect man list of the woman who met 9 out
of ten things on his perfect woman list but, he was in love
with her.
Stretching for a way to make up for that tenth thing.
Like a sprinter, who understands that his stretch could mean
the difference between winning or losing the biggest race of
his life, up until that point, by less than a second.
Or maybe, like me, a multi-tasking man, (yes I know that's
apparently an oxymoron), nonetheless, a man stretching for
multiple personal goals at once; so that I can be the one who
shatters her ideal that a man will hurt her by letting her
down, so that I can be the one that helps her feel what being
part of a happy couple feels like, so that I can be the one
who completes her happily ever after, so that I can be the
one who takes her to her dream destination.
Tirelessly, stretching to be a better man, the…perfect…
man….
Yet, I know, I may never make it to the ten of her list, but
perhaps, if I stretch enough, I can make it to 9.996.
Why six? Because it's more than five and I believe most
people round up after five. And well, six is my favorite
number, and I know that it holds some, however minute,
significance to her, also.

Aaron Paul Mossett

We have that in common.

In truth, we have so much in common, that if I were the perfect man, already, we probably could not grow together; because neither of us would need to stretch.

So yes, I stretch to grow, I stretch for her, I stretch for myself, I stretch for life, I stretch for perfection.

See, the way I understand it, if perfection is slow death, it would have to be longer life.

And if she would round up, I would love to have a long life with her, because she makes me better, she helps me stretch from a 9 to a 9.996 and I could make her better, by allowing her to experience the love that she felt she might never have, thereby allowing herself to love me, and becoming my 9.996.

Then we, stretching together, would be a 19.992, much more than 10,

and therefore much more than Perfect!

Aaron Paul Mossett

Reflections of a Nice Guy...

Notes

Aaron Paul Mossett

O.C.D.

he had compulsions to hug her,
but because of her obsession,
she couldn't allow him in her space;
he had compulsions to kiss her,
but because of her obsession,
she couldn't look him in his face;
he had compulsions to converse with her,
but because of her obsession,
she couldn't hear what he was trying to say;
he had compulsions to forgive her,
but because of her obsession,
remorse was something she couldn't convey;
he had compulsions to make a vow to her,
but because of her obsession,
commitment was something she could not discern;
he had compulsions to love her,
but because he hadn't done her wrong, yet
love was something she could not return.

Aaron Paul Mossett

Reflections of a Nice Guy...

Notes

Aaron Paul Mossett

The Pot

now she's on the button,
while I find myself one of the blind.
I've got at least three choices:
fold, check, or raise, I need to make up my mind.
I know she's willing to take the chance,
though the future she can't foresee,
so I need to be ready to take this gamble,
or abandon it - completely.
should I decide to check,
it's not known how long she'll wait,
can't keep her waiting too long,
I need to fish or cut bait.
can't tell who has the short stack,
at first, I thought I did,
but there's great potential for this pot,
and so she makes her bid
she bets half her stack before the flop,
damn, that move is bold,
but she's confident in the hand she was dealt,
so I must: raise, call, or fold.
calmly, she reminds me,
"I'm a good one, perhaps you forgot,
and though I like you in this game with me,
you have to bet, or get off the pot."
tired of worrying about what I had to lose,
not satisfied anymore with a mere call,
I looked at what I had to gain,
and I went ahead and bet it all.

Aaron Paul Mossett

Reflections of a Nice Guy...

Notes

Aaron Paul Mossett

The Man
Recently I've been considering
The man that is me
The man that I've been
The man I hope to be
I've gone from happy to sad
And then repeated the course
Now I want happy so much
I'm willing to take it by force
I won't joke I've considered
To lie, to cheat, to steal
But I don't want it by such force
I want it by force of will
By such things as the others
I never want to be known for
For there's no honor in those
And I'm capable of much more
I'll be known to be
A good man, good friend, and best dad
A true man of honor
One whose word is ironclad
I want to be the standard
A man everyone wants to know
The man whose forever bragged about by his fellas
And his lady's model beau
The guy that inspires
Whoever may know me
That quality man
Every other man wants to be
To keep to my plan
To satisfy my need
All this can happen
If I become the man that's happy!

Aaron Paul Mossett

Reflections of a Nice Guy...

Notes

Aaron Paul Mossett

eminent domain

he used to have insomnia tic nights.
never happy about dreams deferred.
not content with poetic ideas un-uttered,
for no one heads the unvoiced word.
he wasn't in a good emotional residence, back then.
the result was love unreturned,
the doctrine of self-love reconsidered,
his idea of selfishness unlearned.
training himself to give an inch
where he used to give a mile,
where there used to be grudging concession,
there was now forgiving denial.
his aim was never to be mean,
more so, to protect his mental and emotional health;
because, in the past, after what he gave away.
there was nothing left for himself…
so he learned to enjoy the solitude,
he learned to appreciate the quiet time,
and from the glow of his inner light,
he began to manifest an outer shine.
like moths to a flame,
others sought his glow.
but where old tenants only collected,
finally, he had residents who would also bestow.

Aaron Paul Mossett

Reflections of a Nice Guy...

Notes

Aaron Paul Mossett

Reflections of a Nice Guy...

the invisible man

never fully appreciated
never really shunned
on the list of friends to lean on
never far from number one
soon after the initial "thank you"
his exceptionality was forgotten
he hated being a thing short and sweet
for the taste it left was rotten
soon began his desire
of escaping life like this
he figured that his presence
only a few would actually miss
but before he vanished
he would be less evident
he would began with his disposition
more or less, indifferent
in the proceeding days
he knew friendships would likely sever
but he'd maintain his stoic front,
his attitude was "whatever"
soon he'd have no distinction
be referred to as anon
it didn't even matter to him
if they cared where he'd gone
then the hour arrived
the culmination of his plan
no longer was he the person to count on
he had become the invisible man.

Aaron Paul Mossett

Reflections of a Nice Guy...

Notes

Aaron Paul Mossett

Reflections of a Nice Guy...

I, Outstanding

Recently, I had the desire to become invisible;
not truly understanding the meaning of not being perceived.
It began to feel like I had not existed;
nothing I ventured could, by me, be achieved.
At one point, I could have sworn;
even my prayers were not being received.
People behaved as though I didn't matter.
I felt for a second some conspiracy had been weaved;
woven, by the universe, which was only obliging my mood;
a desire, which I had ill conceived.
The consequences of which, I had misunderstood.
Through that misunderstanding,
my mind wandered and took flight.
Then upon finally landing,
it settled on this specific plight:
What if the invisibility I was demanding
had my universe shook?
Shaken, that request I began countermanding;
so by the universe I would no longer be forsook.
Forsaken, my ignorance of "The Secret" not withstanding;
so I'm running with the idea like a crook.
Before my eyes, my fortune is expanding,
and I am no longer being miss took.
Not mistaken, about my wish to be outstanding;
because now I have a much brighter outlook!

Aaron Paul Mossett

Reflections of a Nice Guy...

Notes

Aaron Paul Mossett

something wicked

had happiness
it was evicted
on account it wasn't paying the emotional bills
decided to play it cold wicked
in that too, I possess mad skills
so now I'm a bad guy
my conscience lifted
as a young man
they called me gifted,
now they ask, "Where's your smile?"
it's been sifted
by losses and deaths, life's rights and lefts
thrown at me this life I've existed
so now I'm a bitter man
I enjoy this evil plan
To it, I may become addicted
Cause I kinda like being
Something Wicked!

Aaron Paul Mossett

Reflections of a Nice Guy...

Notes

Aaron Paul Mossett

Reflections of a Nice Guy...

...this dance?

he was not unattractive,
she'd seen him when he arrived.
she watched him go to the bar,
and come away with white wine.
he was nicely dressed,
wisely groomed, not flashy at all,
he approached a group of ladies;
their backs to the wall.
there were giggles in the exchange,
but they would not be wiled,
he turned away empty-handed,
saw her, and smiled…
she decided then, she'd honor him
she'd give him his big chance,
she thought she'd make his night,
just by favoring him with a dance…

she was a ten in eight's clothing,
he saw when he came in the door,
when he got his drink he felt her looking,
from over there across the floor.
she was sexily dressed,
everything about her just right.
still, he made his way around the place,
he wanted nothing more than a dance, tonight.
he was politely received,
the ladies did him no wrong,
two claimed to be flattered,
but this just wasn't their song.
as he turned, he saw her looking.
he offered her a smile,

Aaron Paul Mossett

she grabbed his hand and led to the dance floor,
he really liked her style…

so they danced all night,
never saying more than one word,
through slow dance and fast beat
their body languages conferred.
By the end of the night,
she was happy about her favor,
lessened, only slightly
by the small note he gave her.
she unfolded the note,
thinking, "I don't think I want any romance."
what she read slightly dismayed her,
these four words, "Thanks for the dance."

Aaron Paul Mossett

Reflections of a Nice Guy...

Notes

Aaron Paul Mossett

Dream Girl

I wanna like a woman so much,
that every kiss is like the first.
I wanna trust her in a manner, in which,
I'd never fear living through better or worse.
I wanna fall in love at each first kiss,
not as a consequence of habit.
Some might think it'll never happen
but if I can imagine it, shit, I can have it!
I wanna have a woman I trust so much,
I can ignore front doors, 'cause she's got my back...
But no matter where we go in this world
she'll always be a true class act.
It's like a total memory recall,
I know she's real 'cause she's in my dreams,
and I may have met the right one,
just not at the right time, it seems…
I imagine a woman so very beautiful,
she'll turn every head in a place.
I mean internally lovely- soul deep,
not just seen when beholding her face.
I wanna feel like opening every door for her,
from now until our heads look snowy white,
I wanna bottle extra hugs for her,
so she'll have them for cold or sleepless nights.
I wanna feel like coming home to her,
just to ask, "Baby, how was your day?"
And I wanna be so deeply into her,
That I'll hang on every word she has to say.
I wanna woman I can love so much,
that I'd happily share my life.
I wanna love her how my step-pops loves my mom,

Aaron Paul Mossett

and proudly announce her as, "My wife!"
I think I have the same to offer,
well except, maybe, for the pretty face,
and as an extra bonus, she'll get to laugh,
two and half of every three days.
One may wonder: "What good is laughter?"
especially, when love can be such a morass.
I believe a laugh brightens up any thing…
Ha ha ha, I just said ass….Oh well,
that's the rough blueprint of my fitting mate,
perhaps a might bit idealistic.
But I'd rather have hope in possibility never realized
Than not believe, and have consequently missed it.

Aaron Paul Mossett

Reflections of a Nice Guy...

Notes

Aaron Paul Mossett

I, Poet

I'm a hopeless romantic,
because I can't be less than passionately chivalrous.
I don't always feature love topics,
sometimes that theme is superfluous.
I don't always wish to rhyme,
probably due to thinking in blank verse;
but some folks won't read the lines,
unless they find the rhythm first.
I be writin' social commentaries,
with a bit of humorous undertone,
I like readers to discuss the contents- What?!
What'dya mean, "I be..." is wrong?
I have written, do write, and will write, again.
It's a habitual progressive,
so in short, "I be writin'."
I've always loved wordplay,
yes, the lexical semantics.
and as the world whirled,
I got better at the dynamics..
I'm like a child weaned on simile,
I like pieces that drip with metaphor.
It must be in my pedigree,
I'm third generation scribbler.
Like the thirteenth warrior,
I can draw sounds.
and speak them back, too!
with adjectives, verbs, adverbs and nouns.
An incurable idealist,
not cardinally amorous,
my passion's for the written word, itself
when my passion's shared, it's glorious.

Aaron Paul Mossett

Reflections of a Nice Guy...

Notes

Aaron Paul Mossett

Reflections of a Nice Guy...

coin toss

events of my life have been tossed up like coins.
on a daily basis, I'm confused about my comings and goings.
every single minute I await a coin's landing;
heads, I can stretch my arms; tails, I have no legs for standing.
these days I have so many things up in the air.
it's more relevant how the wind blows, rather than what's right or fair.
for that reason, I keep my eyes open in these streets, as I'm walkin'.
with the presumption that these same streets, I may need to start stalkin'.
I'm looking for the means to recover from the last loss,
I'm trying to influence my next coin toss.
because I haven't witnessed how the means justify the ends,
my darker side's considering committing sins.
considering turning in professionalism, nice shoes, and three-piece suits,
for the more brutal fit of dark hoodies and black Timberland boots.
evolving from the squirrel collecting nuts, to the wolf stalking prey.
it's more a matter of survival, than the thought of making an easier way.
for being a good guy there seems to be no benefit clause.
since I don't like that effect, I may as well change the cause.
no longer content with room to breathe, I really want some living space.
can't wait for what folks might give; so, I guess I'll go with what I can take.
the stakes are high, but I may have to risk the cost,
guess it all comes back down to one last coin toss...

Aaron Paul Mossett

Reflections of a Nice Guy...

Notes

Aaron Paul Mossett

I Shine

I have been here for thirty-five years, and
I have recently noticed, perhaps by happenstance,
the look of delight on other people's faces when I smile.
If I could put it into words it would say:
"Damn! That's bright!!!"
But they were mistaken to think
that it was the whiteness of my teeth…
Shhh, see one time I had forgotten to brush them.
Some declared it was the twinkle in my eyes,
But, why'd I get the same reaction when I wore shades, polarized
with UV protection, not to mention my tinted contacts?
Even still some of my contacts claimed it might have been the
luminosity of my skin
or shade of my complexion.
Some went as far as to inquire what I'm mixed with…
Nothing, I am Black, well I get darker in the summer…
Perhaps it's because I am disquietingly silent,
and colorfully complex,
that I was able to hear the truth in a friend's wisdom.
As this like souled, well –wisher, who calls me Skippy, used a wish
to grant me the sight of others when they look upon me.
A wish with a desire so strong that right before the bat of my eye
I was able to see what others saw…
I shine…
In fact, I shine so bright I blinked.
Not at the brightness and not at the fear that my shine may intensify
the shun of others;
I blinked at the fear that I shine,
and at the knowledge that I can shine brighter, and brighter, and
brighter, and then brighter again.
See I was feeling kinda somber that day.

Aaron Paul Mossett

Reflections of a Nice Guy...

I knew I had at least four levels of brightness to my base day.
If that is what people see on my dark day, I could not imagine what they might see
on my lightened day, a level-four day, a radiant day.
The universe forbid a day in which I truly felt brilliant…
And because I could not imagine, I could not see…
I blinked… seeing only the afterimage.
But the knowledge was there deep down inside stimulating my inner self like the prompting of a sneeze.
And it had been rising with the pressure of a geyser, unrelieved and waiting for 359,999 years, 11 months, and 2 days, and counting.
Impatiently waiting….
One, five, ten, twenty, thirty, thirty-five
I will be 36 next month, and I see the equation:
36 times 10 to the 4th power equals-- Eschew! Eruption!
I'm about to erupt, y'all! Can you feel it? The energy around me is so palpable it's shimmering.
It's rising and building and anticipating
Starting from here, my core…
It's smiling joyously, sometimes, laughing raucously.
A smile like that first smile 35 years, 11 months, and 27 days ago, when I was welcomed into this existence.
Before my introduction to doubt, disappointment, and defeat;
when a smile was the reaction to the only stimulus I knew:
Love.
When I was fully aware of all the potential that love held.
I smiled…
A smile so wide and so warm it embraced without arms.
That gummy, toothless, close-eyed, sun-absent, wet-skinned smile that roared!
"I am here! People love me here! I love people here!!!"
For that reason,
I shine!

Aaron Paul Mossett

Notes

Aaron Paul Mossett

Drive

now moving at a faster pace
and the going has become turbulent,
I try to keep my focus on the destination
because the reward would be heaven sent.
but my faith alignment is a little off,
so my progress is a bit unsteady.
for this next leap of constancy,
I'm not so sure if I'm ready.
so many times prior
my spiritual engine has stalled…
don't know when or even if
I'll find more divine wherewithal.
perseverance is my sole fuel.
at times, my tank can be found wanting;
the haven is somewhere ahead,
its promise is teasing and taunting.
I can't give up.
therefore, I have no fear.
if it comes down to it,
I'll just shift into a lower gear.
for every beginning I understand
there's an end in the distance.
the best way to get to that point,
is my own octane of perseverance.

Aaron Paul Mossett

Reflections of a Nice Guy...

Notes

Aaron Paul Mossett

Inner Child
I am currently living vicariously,
through my own inner child.
I freed him some time ago,
come see me, and I'll show you how.
Just let me tickle your imagination,
and I can promise that you'll smile.
This will take off five years, or so,
there will be no denial.
Come run, play, and dance with me.
Have some fun and loudly laugh,
minerals in the fountain of youth.
Well, come on, friend!? Take a bath.
We won't overdo it,
because there's one thing I've come to learn:
Once you let the child too far out,
the child will loathe the return.
The balance takes much practice,
I still don't really have it all in check
I have no great responsibilities, though.
Enough adult needed to reason and pay debt.
Yours may be a different circumstance,
Your days may need thought that's more discerning.
I don't have that existence, at this point
and won't fault you for to it, returning.
Nonetheless, you'll have enjoyed the time we had
and you'll want to play, again.
When you do just call on me,
forever and always your play date friend.
Sometimes I may be hard to find,
it's probably 'cause I'm in a bit of trouble.
See, I be playin' in the rain, with my child-like friend,
"Stompin' the shit outta mud puddles!"

Aaron Paul Mossett

Reflections of a Nice Guy...

Notes

Aaron Paul Mossett

Contention

How does my ability to admit my interest in you,
make me an instant contestant in the hard-to-get game?
What makes you that much more an acquisition than I?
Especially, when our game seems the same…
Perhaps, it's the rules that have been established,
for they set you up as the prize…
Well, if you're the blue ribbon that I strive so hard for,
what exactly am I, in your eyes?
And what if, during this event,
I find that I'm as much an acquirement as you?
Would that give me a slight advantage?
More importantly, would you then pursue?
I know your chase may be just a slim chance,
shit, you had such an advantage in this game;
no matter how much harder I compete,
seems the lead you have remains unchanged…
Though the odds, this season, may be stacked against me,
I know my potential hasn't been ignored,
the scouts are even talking co-management, and I'm considering
because, eventually, I won't want to be a player no more…

Aaron Paul Mossett

Reflections of a Nice Guy...

Notes

Aaron Paul Mossett

Que Sera Sera

He'd spent the last year of his life with no relationship ties.
Then he met a young lady, she reunited him with sentimental highs.
Daily, he found himself struggling trying to reduce her spell on his mind,
but the enchantment returned nightly, it was a tie that binds.
Everything delivered her aspect, just like a smell reminds…
He saw her name in all writings, and her face in all designs.
Sometimes he wanted to forget about her, somehow make the clock rewind…
Yet, he responded to all her appeals, and he did it, "time after time".
This luckless young fellow, began to lose his reason to rhyme…
He found himself in a quandary, with a nigh insurmountable climb.
She had absconded with his affection, not quite a victimless crime…
And what a grand theft it was, like filching five hundred dollars, ten dimes at a time.
But he'd never condemn her, for he believed her intentions benign…
So he reappraised his own emotions, and set for his subconscious a high incline.
He spent much time by himself; he was un-resentfully untied…
No principle obligation, or trepidation; no complicated effects on the side.
And whenever he saw whilom flame, he'd greet her cheerfully, smile bona fide…
A fond relationship they maintained, no subject between them would hide.
This was an agreeable contingency, in which their relationship could abide…
And through these experiences, he was finally able to conceive;
that philosophy which taught: Whatever will be, will be…

Aaron Paul Mossett

Reflections of a Nice Guy...

Notes

Aaron Paul Mossett

Urban Samurai

A son of ebony cougars,
he shared a crib with semi-auto Rugers;
they were siblings of neutral intent.
At a young age, politically and socially aware,
by age ten, he knew of reading, writing, even Maoist warfare.
By age fourteen, he'd secretly glanced through Sun Tzu;
but in his world, the Art of War was colored red and blue.
Temperately gangsta, rarely, if ever, thug;
hot when defending a right, cold when avenging a wrong.
Strong senses of intergrity whet his moral code,
considered a man of honor before he was twenty-one years old.
He'd heard the forging of a sword was hard on the forger,
molded by his mother, he understood that to be true,
but as the one being shaped, he perceived the sword's point of view…
After years of being honed and sharpened, to etch his own way in this land;
he resolved the way of the weapon, would be guided by the intent of the man.

Aaron Paul Mossett

Reflections of a Nice Guy...

Notes

Aaron Paul Mossett

no more Mr. Nice Guy

always desiring,
never acquiring,
and therefore he perfected the craft.
the perfect man,
the perfect friend,
fulfilling in all tasks.
the person to lean on,
the shoulder to cry,
but in the back of his head the constant reminder nigh;
"You're just too nice."
observing other men,
studying their routine,
at length he decided; be the exception not the mean.
but change is inevitable,
the adaptable survive,
so he edited, he reread,
and he ultimately revised.
the new he emerged,
with airs of cool relax,
Mr. Nice now well hidden,
by much more attractive masks.
he impressed, excited, delighted, and enthralled
at least 'til the situation grew a little more involved.
older heads have an adage they sometimes relay,
and such was the next act in his life's little play
"what's hidden in the darkness, will soon come to light…"
and so he bore witness to the return of Mr. Nice.
back with a laugh,
and a deep mellow tone,
he flashed his smile,
and they shied from the light shone.

Aaron Paul Mossett

Reflections of a Nice Guy...

afraid and confused,
the roses wilted away.
too much love, too much care, too much nourishment,
caused the decay.
they left too fast,
due to advantages they would seek,
he supposed the women misunderstood;
too nice is not equivalent to weak.
ducking and dodging all attempts to reconcile,
they fled
and Mr. Nice was self-exiled,
my how his heart bled.
now some time later all is done and said,
there is no smile, there is no light
'cause Mr. Nice is dead....

Aaron Paul Mossett

Reflections of a Nice Guy...

Notes

Aaron Paul Mossett

Made in the USA
Las Vegas, NV
26 August 2024

94471944R00090